Whe

Val,
now you will
see the motivation
for my purposes!
He uses
broken
people!
Love!
Cindy

Cindy McFadden

Where is Love ?

Painting on cover is by the author Cindy McFadden, to see more of her art go to cmcfadden.com

Published By
Five Stone Publishing
Potter, Kansas
Five Stone Publishing is a ministry of the International Localization Network

Printed in the United States of America

Where is Love?

Cindy McFadden

Table of Contents

Forward

When I met Cindy McFadden 12 years ago, I was a newbie on the block. My husband accepted the pastorate at Busti Church of God, and we moved our two young children to the lush countryside of western New York. Cindy became the leader of our youth group, and I discovered right away that she was a kid at heart! Cindy led our youth on retreats, mission trips and service to the community. But most of all, Cindy led our youth with her heart, to seek God's heart.

I remember one time in particular, when Cindy asked me to come and speak to the group about reading God's Word. Her desire to nurture their love for the 66 Books of the Bible permeated the types of experiences Cindy provided for the youth. And Cindy didn't just tell them to read their Bibles; she modeled it by being a student of God's Word.

One of the things I have benefited most from is Cindy's prayer life. Cindy has faithfully prayed for me and my family through many seasons of change. I know that for a fact, because she doesn't just say she will pray, but she makes the time for us to pray together. As our friendship grew, her love for art filtered into our prayer times too. Through hikes to Zoar Valley, picnics at Luensman Overview Park, and excursions to Roger Tory Peterson Institute, I have witnessed Cindy's awe of God's creation. That deep respect for

God's world reflects throughout her art, worship, and relationships.

As the passion to share her story grew, Cindy began seeking ways to help others learn from her mistakes. She knew that if her experiences could help at least one other person, then she would have found a way to comfort them too. This book was borne from her many seminars, Bible studies, one-on-one sessions, and prayer for the Lord's direction. I know you will sense Cindy's thirst for God, as you read this chronicle of pain and perseverance. May you also find forgiveness, compassion and healing in the One who alone can fill our love-hunger: Jesus, the Christ.

Sally Ferguson
www.sallyferguson.net
Jamestown, NY

I dedicate this book to my
Maker, my Husband, my Best Friend,
my Soul-Mate and Saviour. Who has
loved me with a Love I never dreamed
could be true.

Cindy

Where is Love?

Chapter 1

I Peter 5:8 - Be self-controlled and alert. Your enemy the devil prowls around like a roaring lion looking for someone to devour.

Children ran, laughed and shouted on the playground beside the elementary school. They played with gusto, for when the school bell rang, playtime would end and school begin.

Like a lost and lonely waif, I stood near the entrance of the stately old building, watching the other kids, wishing I could find a way to be part of the fun. I knew the children; their names, their grade levels, where they lived. But, although I had attended the school since kindergarten, I still, at age nine, didn't feel I was a part of the whole scene. And I was sure the others felt I was a misfit, too. Only two neighborhood friends sometimes called, "Cindy, come and play." I would shake my head and stand alone.

Most of the time loneliness was my only companion. One sunny spring day, a stray dog approached me in what seemed friendly fashion, but when he drew near, he lifted his leg on my foot. Even he felt me worthless.

At home my siblings teased me cruelly. I was low child on the family totem pole and they made sure I knew it. "You're so skinny you could hide behind a flag pole and not be seen at all," they said. Finally, I was so used to ridicule I didn't even fight back. I felt they were right.

There was one place where I felt comfortable. That was in the Sunday school class at church. I loved the wooden, brightly painted chairs. I sang, "Jesus loves me," and I was drawn to the life-sized portrait of Him which hung on the wall. He seemed the most friendly, approachable person I'd ever seen. I wished I could crawl up into His lap and talk to Him. But my respite was always short-lived. As soon as I left Sunday school, Satan managed to turn me back toward sadness.

Most young children are very impressionable and I was no different in that respect. We all have things that shape and mold us in a negative way. That's when the enemy moves in and uses the negative scenario to his advantage. As a teenager, that's where I was, painfully shy, skinny, and lonely. A ripe field, ready for Satan to harvest.

Mel Gibson's movie, "The Passion of the Christ", opens with a scene in the Garden of Gethsemane. Christ is praying for strength to face what is coming. Satan whispers, "You don't really believe one man can die and cancel sin for all men, do you? That's impossible." That must have caused a tremendous struggle in our Savior's soul. The devil always knows where our weak spots are.

Long before Christ's time on earth, Satan talked to Eve in the Garden of Eden. "Did God really say you would die if you ate this fruit? Surely not." And Eve fell for his argument.

We must daily be aware, for he questions us, too. "Did God really say, "No sex before marriage?" Or did He say, "Wear no tattoos"?

When I was a young girl, my family moved to a new neighborhood. This separated me from the kids I was used to. At the same time my parents changed churches. The new one was very large. I felt intimidated by it, but I asked my parents' permission to attend Sunday School there. I was the only one of four siblings who wished to do so.

My mother was a nurse and worked on Sundays, so my dad would drive me to the church, drop me off, and head back home. But Satan tempted me. "You can't go in there. You don't know anyone."

As soon as Dad was out of sight, I threw my offering coins in the neatly trimmed shrubbery and went walking through the downtown section of the city. I'd gaze into store windows and pretend I was shopping on my own. One jewelry store had a large round clock in the window. When I saw it was almost time for my dad to pick me up at church, I'd head back. For a long time no one knew the difference until after several weeks went by, a lady saw me outside the church and invited me in. They were studying the Old Testament, much of which deals with people who are lost and astray. I could relate to that! But to me, the tales of God's people and their wanderings did not seem very real. (It took me 18 more years to come to a real knowledge of God and of His desire to spend time with me.)

When I was in sixth grade, we had a talent show at school. Three of us decided to sing a Roaring '20s song and to do the Charleston. One of the girls' aunt had some original 1920s dresses. One day after school we went up in her hot, dark attic to look through an old, ornate trunk. I found a pretty black lacy dress. We each got a set of long beads and a fancy hat. I thought I was pretty cool. It was a lot of fun spending time with those girls and learning the song and dance. When the time came, we were nervous but everything went well and we were pleased. Then, when it was all over, Carolyn's mom took our pictures and gave us each a 5 x 7 print. I was devastated.

The picture showed Linda on one side of me with her long curly blonde hair framing her face in lovely fashion. Carolyn was on the other side. Her short curly blonde hair was fluffed up in an equally attractive hairdo. My hair looked to me like a dirty, dishwater blonde mess. My bangs were way too short, I had a crooked tooth, and the bright red lipstick I wore showed up in the picture as too dark and too red. My spirits sank.

Granted, this was my subjective viewpoint. We females all seem to have this self-destructive habit. We feel inadequate. It is tempting to believe that we do not measure up. We see as the "norm" the models on television and on magazine covers. But think about this; the average model is 5 feet 8 inches tall, weighs 100 pounds, and wears a size 2. This is nearly impossible for most of us.

The pictures on magazines have been air-brushed, and the models have make-up artists to paint them beautiful. Hairdressers do their hair, and they are helped by having the best lighting possible. No wonder we have a hard time relating to the impossible!

Our enemy, Satan, knows this is a weak spot for all women, and he pushes in. Our insecurity provides a major stronghold for him. He uses it to control us. The world teaches that we must all be beautiful and chic at all times to be acceptable. However, all we have is an embellished, clever wrapper with little substance. We think we don't amount to much. But it is what is inside us in our hearts that really counts. That, and that alone, is what we take with us into Eternity.

Young girls, focus your efforts on what you are on the inside. Are you kind? Forgiving? Friendly? Caring? These qualities form the basis of who you are. Develop yourself on the inside, and the outside will glow with inner joy, with God's glory.

I want to share with you an interesting sidelight on the book of Jonah. Most of us are familiar with the story of Jonah and how he was swallowed by a big fish. God asked Jonah to go to Ninevah to tell the people that God loved them. But Jonah didn't want to go and tell that to the people he hated. The story starts out this way. "The Word of the Lord came to Jonah." He didn't have a Bible. He had to listen for God's voice. He heard the words, but he made a wrong choice. He chose to run away from God instead of obeying Him.

Disaster followed. (It must have been very dark inside that fish's stomach!)

We all have choices. God's Word comes to us, too. We must make decisions all day long beginning with the morning question, "Should I get up?" As a young teen I had only a scrap of God's Word. I had memorized the Twenty-Third Psalm and the One Hundredth Psalm. I'm sure God was trying to get my attention through them but I turned away. Satan was also speaking and I listened to him. Foolishly.

You and I have a choice today. Satan would like to take us captive and make us feel we are nobodies. But God has a dream and a plan for each one of us. We can listen to God or let Satan move in, questioning God's Word.

Dear, sweet, Abba Father, help us to stand firm against the enemy and stay focused on you. Help us listen to You and not Satan who wants to devour us. Through Christ we pray, Amen

Where is Love?
Chapter 2

Jeremiah 29:11 For I know the plans I have for you, declares the Lord, plans to prosper you and not to harm you, plans to give you hope and a future.

Oh, if you could see that today, young people, God truly has dreams and purposes even for the rough times in your life. His number one purpose for you is for you to worship Him and do it no matter what is going on in your life.

Our lives are so short compared to eternity. Remember that, when you are going through rough times. The difficulties will come because this is a fallen world. Jesus Himself, as a human here on earth, had a very difficult life. When we read the Bible, we see no one had a perfect carefree existence. But God and His angels are at work, and there is a plan being carried out.

As a young girl, I knew nothing about sex. Life was very different in the '50s and '60s. Television was innocent and so were a lot of us. Because I was shy and compliant, I was the perfect candidate for young boys to try out their experiments in sexual matters.

At age fifteen I had not dated or had a boyfriend; I had kissed a boy but once and it really didn't go anywhere. Shortly after that along came this young man, tall, blonde and popular. He showed an interest in me. We were walking home one night. It was a warm night and the street lights seemed so bright. It was great to have someone take an interest in me. He leaned down to kiss me right out on the street, and it was exciting! Then he touched me under my clothes. I was shocked and didn't know what to do or what to say. I know it is hard now to believe someone would be that dumb, but I was.

One night I was babysitting. That same guy came over. He had an agenda and I was not aware of it. He wanted to go upstairs and even be on the bed, and you can imagine where this was going; but I was uncomfortable and confused at his wanting to do such intimate things. I am ashamed to say he got his way. Then he left.

This was not the end of it all. Two other boys were part of this plan.

How frightening it was when I answered the door to find another boy I hardly knew. He wanted to use me in the same way as the first boy. I was not stupid. I mustered enough strength to push him out the door. Then a third kid came. By then I must have been in shock, but I sent him away too.

What did I learn from all this? One thing I learned was to have respect for myself. I would wait for a husband I can love and who loves me enough to wait until the wedding.

Jesus gave His all for us, and by remaining pure we can stay holy and give our all for Him. If He is in your life, he lives in your body; and, as the Bible says, "All other sin is outside the body and sex involves the body." We should not abuse Him or our bodies with careless sex.

Now, this brings up a question. Have some of you already gone too far? Even with more than one person? Make a vow right now to God that you will remain clean until your wedding night. You may have heard the term, we are told "everybody does it". But you do not have to do it. I wish with all my heart that someone had taught me this concept of virginity until marriage. It would have saved a lot of pain in my soul.

The thing we need to realize is that when we are sinning in a sexual way, it truly separates us from God. He is holy. Not all boys are like these whom I mentioned, but you need to watch out for the ones who are. My so-called boyfriend never spoke to me after that one encounter.

As young women, you need to be ready to say "No" to this kind of conduct. No one has the right to use you without your consent. I had not been shown or told of all the places in God's love letter, the Bible, that sex before marriage is WRONG. The Apostle Paul said to flee from sexual sin. It is only for the marriage bed. Boys will say they love you. But do they love and respect you enough to wait for marriage? I pray the best for you.

I can only imagine what it's like to be pure and to have experienced on my wedding night true oneness and true intimacy with my husband. I know all through history there were slipups, but until my generation we treated sex in God's way. My generation, the hippies or baby boomers, promoted free love, or love wherever and whenever. I see how this has destroyed and changed our society. Back then, I did not know one person who was divorced or who came from a divorced family.

You see, the Word of God says you become one when you have sex. One survey says the average bride and groom have had 10 lovers. So when they come to their wedding night, there is nothing unusual or exciting or intimate about it.

With God in your life, you can right this. For example, there was a young girl who lived with us for eight years. I helped her invite Jesus into her life. I convinced her to be pure from then on. She had made mistakes in the past, but God gives second chances to contrite hearts. I helped her to see things God's way. She prayed and waited on God. And He brought her a wonderful Christian man. They stayed pure until their wedding night. I know God has truly blessed their obedience to him. They have a bond and an intimacy that many young people will never know.

We all need a close relationship with someone. But a friendly close relationship takes time to grow. With couples, the engagement period is a good time for this. Learn each other's morals and values. (You might even find that you don't want to marry this person!) Having fun together, learning to talk things over, even fighting are things that bring closeness. During the engagement period, all of these help a couple build a lasting connection. When we take a shortcut to intimacy, we lose a great deal. When we learn to love the right way, we develop a respect for and an appreciation of our future mate.

Notice the verse at the beginning of this chapter. God has plans for your good and He offers a hope to keep you going. Your future is an open book to God. If you ask, He will guide you into the best possible life patterned carefully to match exactly who you are.

Before I end this chapter, I want to say there are plenty of boys who are good, boys who won't push you to do things you do not want to do or understand. There is nothing more romantic than a godly boy who just wants to be your friend and treats you as a treasure.

Heavenly Father, Thank You for having plans and a purpose for us and a future for Your children. Help us, guide us, give us the strength to stand firm. We need Your blessings. We give You our obedience to Your laws as You enable us. We praise You, great King. In Jesus' name, Amen

Where is Love?

Chapter 3

John 10:10 The thief comes only to steal and kill and destroy. I have come that you might have life and live it to the full.

By the time I was sixteen, I had several guys who wanted me for only one thing. The devil tempted me, but I resisted. The enemy just kept pushing me, over and over.

Then, one fall night at a high school dance, I was introduced officially to a young man named Billy McFadden. I had seen him around, had even been in the same class with him. He was cute and popular, and was from a family well known in the community. He asked me to dance and then walked me home. He asked if I could go to a fraternity dance a couple of weeks away.

I had noticed Billy in our ninth grade art class. The teacher had assigned a project in clay. I worked hard on mine. I made a small bust of a young woman. She had her hair up in a bun, so I worked painstakingly on her ears and of course on her eyes, nose and mouth.

The teacher had said, "When you work with clay, get all the air out of it. It is necessary to pound the clay to eliminate any trapped air or it will blow up in the kiln." Billy had purposely left air in his project. Just as the teacher had warned, it blew up. He had made a round bomb with a wick in it. Of course it blew up my project, too. All my hard work gone.

That incident should have warned me about what I was getting into, but I said I would go to the dance. Those awesome blue eyes and his smooth personality were hard to resist. Like all sixteen-year-olds, I was vulnerable. Actually I had a date with someone else, but I called and gave an excuse to get out of it. I did not know the dance was a Sadie Hawkins dance. We took part in role playing (it involved couples marrying), and Billy and I got "married". It was the beginning of what turned into a forty-year up-and-down relationship for us. In just a month Billy and I were doing things the wrong way. Up until then I was an ideal child, but this new turn was making problems in my relationship with my mom. I think that somehow she knew I was being intimate with Billy. At sixteen I didn't even know what love was nor did I know the author of love then. I didn't know that God's way in a boy-girl relationship is to get to know each other well and so build a firm foundation for either friendship or marriage. Back then, as it often is now, couples just jumped into bed first.

As I write this I am again overcome with shame at all the lies we told our parents just so we could be together. I see now that God's Word says we become one when we have sex. Becoming one is a picture of a covenant or promise in which there is always blood involved. With a virgin, sex always involves blood. When kids today ignore God's Word, we see couples saying, "It's O.K. We'll get married when the time is right." Too often the time just never becomes right and the relationship crumbles into dust. Each moves on to a new partner and the sin continues. They begin to feel like a nothing, as though no one will ever really love them. And Satan is filled with glee.

One time at a conference, I heard a young man say he had treated sex carelessly. Then, later, when he entered into a new relationship, he realized the error he had made. In the new situation he remained pure. He said, "With my new girl friend, I am getting to know her better as a person, and we will have a better foundation for marriage." Is it really any surprise that God's way is the best? He wants very much for us to have the very best in life.

My parents tried to separate Billy and me, but we snuck around even more until we got caught. My parents threatened to send me to live with my aunt in Erie, PA. I panicked and swallowed a bunch of aspirins and a glass of water. As I was trying to go to sleep I remember thinking, Is there really a Hell? Am I going there? I called out to my mom and told her what I had done. She was due at a meeting. She called the doctor who told her, "Make her drink milk. That will cause her to throw up," and it did. I was miserable, but my dad stayed by my side at the toilet and I got rid of the aspirin.

I didn't know it then but I realize now that Satan truly wants to steal our lives so we cannot live in freedom.

Shortly after that incident I realized I was pregnant. It was my senior year in high school. I made an elaborate plan in which I would graduate, go live with a friend, keep the baby, and then go to beauty school.

My mom seemed to have the sixth sense that most mothers do. She snooped in the trash and found that I was wrapping up clean tampons, that I was not menstruating. My life blew up. Our parents talked, and it was decided I would be sent to a home for unwed mothers in Erie after my graduation. I was seven months' pregnant at graduation. I went to the prom in an empire waist dress as well as a girdle, and no one knew my plight. Only God could have seen me through my exams and all that I had to do to graduate. I wasn't a great student. Even in my junior year my mom had gone to the guidance counselor to ask that I be placed in the lower level studies because she said, "She isn't college material." But I did make it.

At the home in Erie I found twenty or more girls in the same situation that I was. I had a great roommate. She was from a nearby town. She, too, had gone to school with the baby's father. Neither of us was happy. We were scared. One night one of the girls lost her baby, and we were ready to panic.

I was the only girl who was visited by the baby's father. Once Billy and his dad came to see me. His father was very kind. We went out to eat at a restaurant. His dad sat on the other side of the restaurant so Billy and I could talk freely. Billy gave me a pretty pearl necklace. Billy often called me and sent me letters. My parents came to visit me once, and it was a very strained situation but they stood by me. I have often thought as I became a grandmother it must have been hard for my parents to encourage me to give up the baby, their first grandchild, for adoption. I now realize what I did to them.

My spirits perked up briefly when my sister-in-law sent me a maternity outfit. It was cute with flowers on the shirt to match the green shorts.

For me, my stay at the home was just a time of unreal existence as though I were walking in a nightmare. I lived just to get through each day. All of us were waiting out our terms.

A social worker visited me a few times to talk about the baby's future. She knew how my parents felt and I had no other resources. I would have to abandon my child, handing him/her over to strangers. And I would have to sign a paper giving up my rights, allowing the adoption. This was before the age of sonograms, so I didn't even know what sex my child would be.

God continued to be good to me even when I did not see Him working. He gave me an adult friend, Shirley. She lived in Erie and was a volunteer at the home. I met her at a picnic at the beach on Lake Erie. I was still pretty new, still in a daze.

I remember sitting alone on a tree stump a short ways up the beach from the lake. Shirley came over and started talking to me. It was the beginning of a great relationship, although Shirley got in trouble for it. The volunteers were not to get too closely involved with the girls or show any favoritism. I enjoyed Shirley. I was invited to her house for dinner and there I met her husband and two sons. I even gave a couple of art lessons to her husband. But we were forced to revert to a volunteer/resident relationship, and Shirley was severely reprimanded. After I left the home I stayed in touch with her. I often tried to tell her how much her friendship had meant to me at a very difficult time in my life. She was humble about it, but I think she was truly God-sent.

The fateful day of my child's birth finally came. One evening after dinner my pains started. My roommate and I went to tell the house mother. She was watching TV. She gave us instructions about timing the pains and told us to come back when the pains grew closer and lasted longer. At about 10:00 p.m. I was taken to St. Vincent's Hospital. My mom was notified. Ironically, my aunt from Erie was visiting her in Jamestown at the same time. She was not aware of my pregnancy, so Mom left the house on some pretext and came to be with me. Before she arrived, the nurse kept checking on me and they made preparations for my baby's arrival. I felt very alone, separated from home and friends and of course from Billy. Isn't this the time the baby's father is supposed to be on hand, be supportive, help his child arrive safely? And isn't this the time when your mother is supposed be on hand?

When Mom, who was a nurse, arrived, she talked them into sedating me so I wouldn't remember anything. The next day I woke up in the recovery room. My mom was there, and I asked about my baby. It was a girl. I wanted desperately to see her but Mom said "No." I begged the nurse to bring her to my room so I could see her and hold her. What a precious bundle she was! When you look at your firstborn, it is a very special and momentous time. I wished Billy could be there with me. He did come to see me and he too thought our child was special.

When it was time to name the baby, I chose to call her Michelle Lynn. How I wished I could keep her and enjoy her forever. But I knew I couldn't.

After a few days I went home and kept my big secret. From time to time as I encountered a special friend, I would tell about my experience. It always made me cry. Mom never talked about it, and at times I had to pretend it had never happened.

Back then, New York State law said newborns like mine must remain in a foster home until they were five months old before they could be "adopted out". During that five months' time I wondered how she was; if she was healthy, if she could smile or turn over or laugh. Did she know I loved her?

Billy was at college in Colorado. I missed him a lot. One day Mom took me to an appointment. Alone, I went upstairs in a creepy old building in downtown Jamestown to sign the adoption papers. They escorted me into a dingy room where the social worker held my Michelle. She was all dressed up with a pink bonnet and a pink coat to match. She was adorable. I was not allowed to hold her. A lawyer was present, and I was instructed in what I was to do. I signed away my baby to someone I did not even know.

When the horror was over, I walked out of the office. The hallway was dark and cold. It smelled musty. It matched my feelings exactly. I walked down endless flights of stairs and onto the street. Mom was waiting at the curb in the car. Neither of us said a word. She never asked a question, never spoke of it again. It was as if it had never happened, as though tiny, precious Michelle Lynn was wiped from the earth.

Billy and I continued to stay in touch. When he came home from college for the summer, our parents worked hard to keep us apart, but we managed to sneak away to be together anyway. My mother said she would have to send me to my aunt in Erie if we didn't stop. We didn't, and she did send me away.

One day while my parents were working, Billy raided their mailbox and copied my address from a letter I wrote to them. He phoned me a couple of times.

I lied to my aunt and slipped out several times to see Billy. My aunt was trying to get me to date some of the boys she knew. I tried to do what she and my parents wanted me to do. I dated one boy who was very nice and not interested in any sexual contact. I told him the story of Michelle, and we became just friends. Billy found out about it and was very upset. There wasn't much he could do about it because he was just about to go back to college in Colorado.

I was still living under a black cloud of guilt and unhappiness, missing Billy and wondering about Michelle. Still, I prepared to go to art school in Pittsburgh.

I had two roommates while in Pittsburgh, one from Jamestown and one from nearby Warren. One of the girls had a boyfriend. He rented a room in a hotel, and we all went there and had a party. I remember not talking much and drinking a lot. I walked out onto the balcony thinking about Billy and Michelle, and I was truly miserable. I thought seriously about jumping over the wrought iron railing to get away from life. I just didn't want to live anymore. I thought about the time I had tried suicide with the aspirins. Even then the enemy was trying to make me feel like nothing. He held me captive, thwarting my God-given purpose as he often does. That's how he got the first people God ever made to disobey their Creator. And to this day he continues to tempt us, too.

Thank goodness, something (Someone?) stopped me from jumping. I'm glad He did because although I didn't know it at the time, I was pregnant again. I realize now, I might have killed two of us.

Dear Heavenly Father, thank You for sparing my life. I know that we are in a spiritual battle and the enemy is alive and well. Thank You for showing me Your purpose for my life Thank You for showing me that You made me in my mother's womb and You are using me for Your purpose. Amen

Where is Love?
Part II - Compassion

Chapter 4

II Chronicles 16:9 For the eyes of the Lord range to and fro throughout the earth to strengthen the hearts of those who are fully committed to Him.

I was in captivity with Satan's power over me, thinking I was nothing, with no purpose in life. I know now that God was just waiting for me to show some interest in Him, that I would come back to Him. But He didn't push me.

When I found out I was pregnant again, I immediately wanted to go to Billy. Although I had very little experience in travel on my own, I bought a plane ticket and off I flew to Denver. First, though, I called the president of the art school where I was still a student, and explained to him what I was doing. I asked him to stall my parents briefly if they should call, trying to locate me. Graciously, he agreed, if I promised to call my parents as soon as I connected with Billy. I agreed and boarded the plane.

I was scared. What if Billy didn't want to see me? What if he blamed me for saddling him with another baby? How would we survive? And yet, deep in my heart, I knew he would help me. When we landed, Billy was not there. I could have panicked, but I stuffed down my worry and waited. When he finally came, we went to his apartment where I met his three roommates. They were kind and tolerated my presence although some time later I found in one of their magazines a sketch of me as a very pregnant lady. It did nothing for my self-esteem. I never figured out which of the boys had drawn it.

I cooked and cleaned for the five of us, but all the time I was very uncomfortable about the whole situation. Billy was almost overwhelmed by it all. He was expected to be a husband and a father as well as a student, all at the age of nineteen. He wanted to complete the final three years of college, but how to do it?

We had called our parents soon after I arrived in Denver. Billy's father was really angry. He said, "I intended to pay for your college years, but now that you have messed up your life again, I will not pay for anything more." Billy was even more upset when he heard that. However, after a time his dad agreed to continue to pay for Billy's college tuition and housing but that was all. The rest was up to us.

We rented a studio apartment. I had to get a job. So did Billy. I saw an ad for a car hop at a nearby restaurant, and I walked down the street to apply. A cadillac pulled up beside me and a man with a big cigar spoke to me. "Where are you going, young lady?"

I naively answered, "I'm going to apply for a job at the restaurant right over there."

The man got out of the car and said, "I own that building right next to it. Want to work for me?" I looked across the street. On top of the building was a mannequin turning around and around in the breeze. I felt uncomfortable, and rightly so, for his place was a strip joint.

I said, "I'm pregnant. I wouldn't do well there."

He replied, "That's okay. You can still strip for me."

As I write this, I can see how easily girls can get sucked into evil things like that. The man was nicely dressed with a fancy car, and he seemed to care about me. I thank the Lord that I had the good sense to say, "No, thank you." And turn away.

I got the job as a car hop. (I would take orders from the customers parked outside the restaurant and deliver them to their cars. I guess you could say it was "Pre-drivethrough" days.)

I found it funny when I thought about it; a car hop dressed in the fancy clothes they provided, a visual made to attract customers. Only they didn't know I was pregnant.

Billy got a job at a fine German restaurant. He worked hard and became the head bus boy. We didn't make much money but we were in love and as happy as we knew how to be.

We were married by a judge in downtown Denver. We both wore jeans and our matching blue toggle jackets. We used a wedding ring Billy had bought for fifteen dollars. The "wedding" was a far cry from what I had long looked forward to. When I was young I had a beautiful bride doll, and like all young girls I had dreamed of a fancy wedding with all my family and friends around me to celebrate. Instead we had no bridal showers, no wedding gifts, no fancy food or well wishers. We didn't even have the basics. Somehow in our innocence, we had thought all that was somehow irrelevant because we were in love.

One day we received a notice from the Post Office. There was a package there for us. We would have to come and pick it up. We had no transportation except a motorcycle, so we walked to the Post Office. We picked up a huge box sent by his mother. At the apartment we opened it to find pots, pans, cookbooks, and a whole batch of kitchen utensils. Now we could cook.

We soon learned that the fairy tales we had enjoyed as children were lies. Marriage is not a "happily ever after" experience. We found that marriage can be difficult, and that it has many seasons. Not all are romantic. Just having a man and a woman living in the same space can be difficult. We communicate in different ways, we have different habits, different perspectives, and have been part of two different dysfunctional families. Newlyweds need to be prepared and not panic when the road to bliss suddenly branches off into a road full of speed bumps. Life's especially hard when you try to live it without God, and we had hardly had a chance to really know each other.

For us, part of the problem was stress. Billy was trying to finish his college courses, meet the demands of his job, and learn how to live with a baby underfoot. He had hoped to become a doctor but changed his mind to concentrate on a business career. Through the years I have come to believe that is what God had gifted Billy for, and he has done well.

Going from life in a small town in upstate New York to life in Denver, Colorado, was certainly an eye opener. Most of our friends were playing around with drugs. It was the late '60s. The university president was quoted as saying, "Ninety percent of the students here have at least tried drugs." Billy and I did experiment, and I remember one night when I was high on hash I hallucinated. Billy kept trying to calm me down, but I was sure that a bear was clawing me to death and then I thought Billy was trying to choke me. And later, some of our neighbors while high on LSD drove up into the mountains, leaving behind their one-year-old baby alone in her crib. That scared me.

Fortunately, my experience with hash was after I had my second child, and I did not use it at all while I was pregnant. Even then, God's fingerprints were on my shoulder.

Kerry Ann had decided to be born at the time of Billy's final exams. We went to the Presbyterian Hospital in the middle of the night. She came so fast the doctor didn't get there on time. I had packed a goodie bag for Billy in case he had to stay with me a long time. And he was so concerned for me, he offered me a cigarette, even though I didn't smoke! But his concern was comforting to me. It was great to have him with me this time.

We had not had any classes or birthing training and had no parents around to guide us. But we made it, and we had another girl. She helped fill the spot in my heart that had been empty since losing Michelle.

I was excited when we brought her home. I wish we had some family or friends around to share our joy. I marvel that God's fingerprints continued to appear from time to time. A church family would have been helpful just then. We had no family, no church, no Bible, no Christian friends. Still I kept running from God even as He pursued me.

At the end of three months I had to go back to work. I had been nursing Kerry Ann and enjoyed the closeness it gave us. But I had to give it up, much as I hated to, in order to hold up my end of the financial burden. Billy worked extra hard at his studies so he could graduate early and begin his career. He wanted to support his family. All of this took time away from our own relationship, but that was part of the responsibility of marriage. I must say I missed being number one in his life. At least that is the way I felt. And I was especially lonely when Billy sometimes went hunting in the mountains on weekends. I guess the old adage is true: "A man gets you to the altar and when that is accomplished, he goes on to concentrate on his own work goals."

When Kerry Ann was about a year old, I had a strong desire to have a son. Almost exactly a year later, I got my wish. I am reminded that God's Word says, "He gives us the desires of our hearts."

Shortly after our son was born, Billy graduated from college, and began a job search. At one point he considered a job selling for Standard Oil Company as a traveling salesman. He also talked to his dad about a job at his car dealership. His dad said, "You can work for me at a later time, but I want you to work a couple of years for someone else first." But he did get a job for Billy with a friend of his in our home area. So, we packed up and moved across the country in a big truck. We found an apartment in a college complex which was near Billy's work.

Even as I write this, I realize that I was in bondage, even as the Hebrews were in bondage to their enemies. I have heard that you are either a Christian belonging to God, or you are a slave of Satan. I was a captive. I didn't choose either one, but like the default setup on your computer, I had not chosen God and so I was automatically on the other side.

I didn't see anything wrong with drugs even when I was pregnant with my third child. It was the '70s and all the warnings about drug abuse had not yet come out. Or at least I had not heard them. I didn't smoke and I didn't do much pot, but again, looking back, I see where God's loving hands were on my life. He put up with the rebellious Israelites for forty years in the wilderness. I am glad I didn't have to stay in my wilderness that long. God is gracious even to sinners.

Billy was working twelve and thirteen hours a day. He wanted to be the best salesman at the dealership. The "happily ever after" continued to dissipate. Billy started bringing home a single guy with whom he worked. I was not happy with the lack of attention from Billy. This visitor paid more attention to me than my husband did.

I understand now that when you don't know God's better plan for marriage and you have engaged in sex with multiple partners, marriage isn't a sacred thing anymore. I often said to myself, "Where is my knight in shining armor?" My life felt empty.

After a year in Rochester, New York, Billy wanted to go back to Colorado. So once more we packed up our things and took our kids across the country. There, some new friends who were customers of Billy's had moved to Colorado before we did. We stayed with them for a few days until Billy got a job and found a small house for us to rent.

I loved that little house! It had a big front yard. I put down sod on the side lawn and fenced it in so the children could play there safely. We lived in the city of Denver, and it was very different for me. I wasn't used to driving in heavy, fast traffic, and I hated driving on the expressway. The noise bothered me, too. And sometimes when we got stuck in a line of traffic, bumper to bumper, I'd get very tense.

Once more, Billy began working day and night. I was very lonely. On weekends Billy often went hunting or fishing in the mountains or in Wyoming.

I began to think about that guy back in Rochester, fantasizing about being with him. I didn't realize then as I do now that God could fill my every need. He wants to be my supplier, my protector, and my lover, just as every good husband would. But I did my own thing, even as Jonah did. In contrast, Billy was human and imperfect, as we all are. God is all-inclusive but Billy isn't. Neither was I able to fill all of Billy's needs. He needed God, too.

I didn't know God created me to have a personal relationship with Him. I didn't know that He longed to spend time with me. Someone has said, "Every girl wants to be lovely and worth pursuing." I didn't know yet that God, the Creator of the universe, was pursuing me. I felt very empty and lonely, with no place to go.

My dear, sweet sovereign Lord. Thank You for creating me for a relationship with You. Thank You for allowing me to feel that emptiness because it caused me to pursue You. In Jesus' name, Amen.

Where is Love?
Chapter 5

Psalm 103:2-5 Praise the Lord, O my soul, and forget not all His benefits. Who forgives all your sins and heals all your diseases, who redeems your life from the dead, crowned you with love and compassion, who satisfies your mouth with good things, so your youth is renewed like the eagle's.

God was pursuing me although I was not even aware of it. I began to do little creative projects, like carving a piece of wood or stitching a seam, even sewing some little things for Kerry Ann. But inside I kept thinking about God the great Creator. He was calling me just as He did so many in His word.

He used one of my new friends, Margaret, who invited me to a Bible study. I agreed to go although I was not sure just what to expect. We would have a project first taught by an expert, like the woman who showed us how to do beadwork. Then we would have a snack with coffee while doing a Bible study, finally, we would pray.

I got really close to Margaret and even told her about Michelle. Our children were about the same age, and they would play together. All in all, I enjoyed our second time in Denver.

One day, Billy came home from work and he got upset about some trash in back of our neighbor's house. Billy wanted me to go talk to them about it. I didn't really want to, and we got into a terrible fight. I ended up crying. Billy stormed out, where to I didn't know and didn't much care.

I was upset and angry with Billy. I finally bundled up Kerry Ann and Bud and called a taxi to take us to the bus station. I bought a ticket to Rochester, and the three of us headed back east to New York State.

On part of the bus ride, two young men came aboard. They were friendly to talk with and they seemed like nice guys. All the time however, I was worrying, desperate, wondering what I was going to do once we arrived in Rochester. Finally, I asked one of the young men if I could live with him. (How desperate we are when we are without God.) Fortunately he turned the talk to something else.

When I got to Rochester I found a hotel; and after the children were asleep, I called Jerry, the single fellow who had often come home with Billy when they worked together. I said, "I'm in Rochester. Could we meet?"

He came over with a bottle of wine; and after we had talked for a while, he decided to spend the night. What a picture of being lost in the wilderness of sin. I was a slave in captivity, unaware of what I was doing to my life.

The next day when Jerry left, I called Billy and told him where I was and what had taken place. He said, "Get a plane and come home right now."

After some serious thought I decided I should go back. How would I support the kids on my own? So we flew back to Denver.

When I got home, Billy and I fought again. Billy said, "Just get out. Leave the kids with me. I don't want you any more." He stormed out. Was this the end of my marriage?

I could see my life unraveling. How did I get into this situation? I cried all night. I finally pulled myself together. I left the kids with Margaret, my friend and neighbor who loved kids. She promised to watch for Billy and turn my darlings over to him.

For some strange reason I kept thinking of Santa Fe. I didn't know why, or at least I did not know at that time. I didn't even know where it was, nor did I know anyone there. Now, years later, I am sure it was God who had plans for me that I did not know about nor would I have understood back then.

In Santa Fe I got a room in a hotel. After leaving my suitcase in the room, I went out to walk. I walked until I was out of the city. I was in a mental fog, looking, searching for meaning. I knew I couldn't go to my parents. They had given up on me when I married Billy. They had never liked him. Between my wrong choices and their dislike for Billy, they had closed the book on me. As I walked along the street, I saw a young man standing nearby. He was wearing a pony tail. It was the standard hairdo for guys back then in the '70s. I walked up to him and asked, "Do you know where

I could get a job or find a place to stay?" He looked a little stunned but finally replied, "I don't know about a place to stay, but maybe a job." He pointed to a van standing at the curb. "These are my wheels. Come with me." I got into the van with him. It was an awfully stupid move. Whether out of innocence or desperation I don't know. Or it may have been God's hand on me-again-keeping me from harm.

Josh was a gentleman and took me to see his friend, Don. We found him at his dining room table with a Bible open in front of him. I had hardly been there a couple of minutes when he said, "Are you saved?"

I hesitated. I had barely any knowledge of that phrase, just that it had to do with church. I knew I had sung in the choir and I had attended Sunday School. That ought to classify me as born again. So I replied, "Sure."

Don started telling me about his life as a drug addict and an alcoholic. He had almost lost his marriage when someone helped him to find Jesus Christ. It turned his life completely around. He told me that he and some friends had formed a Bible study. He was the leader. He asked if I would like to attend. Again I said, "Sure."

Don and Josh took me back to my hotel. I called Billy and told him I was in Santa Fe and that was it. I told him I was really confused. That night I slept with a Gideon Bible under my arm like a teddy bear.

Don and Josh picked me up the next day to go to the Bible study at Don's house. We all sat on the floor of a very large room. Don played a guitar and they all sang choruses I did not know. Then he opened his Bible and taught the lesson. It was on faith. Then they prayed for several people whom I did not know. They prayed in particular for a man named Bob. They hoped he would come to a personal relationship with God. I began to cry. Those Christians gathered around me and talked to me about Christ. But they didn't go into any detail about how one can know Christ. I had said I was a Christian so it never occurred to them to tell me how to have a personal relationship with the Lord.

I spent Thanksgiving with Don, his wife, and three children. He told me that several people in the last year had just showed up on his doorstep. I knew that included me. I took part in the conversation, but I did not tell him I had a husband and children. I guess I didn't want him to know how badly I had failed everyone.

A few days later I was having lunch with a couple of my new Christian friends. I suddenly looked up. There stood Billy! I blinked my eyes and stared at him. He and his college roommate, Greg Brown, were standing in the doorway. Greg had talked Billy into coming to find me.

They came over, and I introduced them to my friends. They were surprised because I had not told them anything about myself. We all talked and laughed, and the awkward gap was bridged.

Later I took Billy to meet Don at his Christian book store. I told Don a little about us. He prayed with us and gave us a Bible. That night Billy and I read from it and talked about it. We felt we had turned a corner.

The journey back to Denver seemed like a long trip, but it felt good to be with Billy. When we got home we found a counselor who was helpful, and soon we were going to church.

Things were slowly improving, but Billy soon decided we should go home again to Jamestown. His dad agreed to hire him but he said, "You can work for me, Bill, but you have to sell and work your way up."

We rented a house for a few months until we found a house we were willing to buy. It was great to have our own home. Billy worked hard and I had my two beautiful children to keep me busy. Life should have been good, but still too often I felt empty and lonely. I didn't know that I was searching spiritually, and there was no one to help me.

One day I answered a knock at the door and found two young men eager to talk to me. I invited them in. These two people identified themselves as Mormons. Their message interested me. They began visiting us regularly. After a while Billy and I became uncomfortable with their message, so Billy went to their apartment and got angry with them before they finally left us alone.

In my heart I had sensed a need for God, and these people claimed to know Him but their view of Jesus Christ did not seem to relate to the Jesus I had heard about.

As I look back over my life, I see myself in a situation very similar to Jonah's. Remember Jonah? He was down in the dark, dark belly of a big fish, and here I was, really kind of in a dark place also not really knowing how to get out. I was trapped. I had no real

ties to God. I had no place to go, no spiritual resource.
I was very lonely. I was homesick for Santa Fe and my
Christian friends.

*Father, thank You so much for caring about me,
for helping me to meet those Christians in Santa Fe.
You reached down to me. I did not know You had a
greater plan for my life. Please help those who have
not yet realized who You are. Lead them to Yourself
just as You led me. Thank You for Your love. Amen*

Where is Love?
Chapter 6

John 3:7 You should not be surprised at my saying you must be born again.

After the Mormons were out of our lives, that empty feeling came back in. I was still going to my childhood church, but it seemed empty and placid. In the summer the two churches of the same denomination would combine for services. We went to one church in July and the other in August.

A couple of Sundays I went to the other church and took my Kerry Ann and Bud. They were about 8 and 6 years old now. When I took the children to junior church, all that was available was nursery through sixth grade all in one room. My children were the only ones there. Then I went upstairs and there was nothing but older people. It felt so empty, and I began to think there had to be somewhere that church meant more to people, even in the summer.

I noticed that there was a church up the hill from our home, and it had three services even in the summer. There were two in the morning and an evening service. One Sunday I decided to give it a try. The people were very friendly and I saw a few that I knew. They had several Sunday School classes and even some for adults. They were studying things that I had never heard before, such as, "You can have a personal relationship with God." I specifically remember a lady singing a solo about there being a hole in your heart. The words said that the hole could not be filled with money, things, people, vacations or jobs. Only Jesus can fill the empty space.

I heard them talk about the fact that we all sinned and fall short of God's mark. We have to repent, and these things started getting into my head and heart and making sense.

It was explained that you have to confess what you have done wrong and ask God to forgive you. He will come into your heart. After going to church for most of my life and now at 27 years of age, I am hearing these things for the first time! As a teenager I would cry as I took communion. I knew there was more to it but I didn't know what.

One night all by myself, I got on my knees beside my bed and asked Christ to forgive me and to come and live in my heart. I didn't feel any different, but I saw some changes right away. I gained more patience with my children, and my language changed. I noticed when people used God's name as a swear word, it made me cringe. It began to hurt to hear them throw His name out like it was nothing.

I was very blessed because I was in a church that had a class for new believers. I had been reading a little devotional for years but never read through the Bible. I tried to read it a few times, but I couldn't understand it. God's Word says that when we come to Him, the Holy Spirit comes in and He is our teacher. Shortly after becoming a believing Christian, I was offered a chance to go to the Holy Lands. I remember thinking I haven't read the Bible, I need to read it. I started at Genesis, and I can't say I understood everything, but things started to become clearer and I began to see how things fit as I was reading through Matthew and coming to chapter 27:51 where it says, "At that moment the curtain of the temple was torn from top to bottom." The Holy Spirit helped me to understand that Jesus had just died and the next sentence says the curtain was torn. I remembered reading in the Old Testament all about the high priest and all that he had to go through and he could only go into the Holy of Holies once a year. Wow, the light went on. Jesus made a way at the time of His death for us as believers to come into the Holy of Holies any time, just come on in.

The whole Bible indicates that God created us and wants a relationship with us. Jesus came to show us who God is, and He died to give us 24/7 access to God's throne. James 5:11 says, "The Lord is full of compassion and mercy." Yes, the Lord had compassion even for me.

At a recent retreat, a Walk to Emmaus I heard it said, "Anything God commands of me is so that my joy may be full and so I will be a target of His blessings." Yes, this is true. As Christians we will have problems, but God is always there and we can have joy in spite of what is going on around us.

Church became very important to me. I wanted to learn and get more. I got involved right away with teaching. I was on the board at the YWCA, and they wanted to start a Bible study. I was to be the teacher. I remember wanting to teach, and that isn't my personality but God was calling me. We will discuss that in the next section. When I think back, it blows me away at how gracious and compassionate God is. He let me, this ignorant, shy new Christian, teach a Bible study class. I learned right away that teaching a class about the Bible is a good way to learn.

One day a nun came to the class. That made me feel quite inadequate, but Sister Sharon actually became my friend.

After leading at the "Y"for a couple of years, I started teaching a class of 3-and 4-year-olds at my church. A couple of years later I began working with high school students. I found I could relate to them and they could relate to me.

In comparing this segment of my life to Jonah's, I see God had compassion on him and made the big fish spit him out and gave Jonah another chance to obey Him. God forgave me, too, and set me on a right path with Him.

We are all lost in the wilderness before we come to Christ. The whole time the promised land is there waiting. I believe Heaven begins the minute we accept Christ. I have always said, "I would never go back to being without Christ for even a second." Now after almost 30 years of walking with Him, I see bits of Heaven and I can't even imagine where I would be without Him. For starters, I'd probably be divorced and alcoholic, and maybe I'd even be addicted to drugs and living a promiscuous life.

Do you realize there are over 7,000 promises in the Bible? One of my favorites is in Philippians 1:6 where it says, "Being confident of this, that He who began a good work in you will carry it on to completion until the day of Christ Jesus!" God wants to connect with us, but He gives us a free will. He has good works and purposes designed just for us as individuals! God promises to carry them out until He returns. To think I was wandering around without a plan or purpose for 27 years seems like such a waste. I am grateful for those people who cared enough to pray for me to finally find Christ. Some I may not meet until I get to Heaven.

Lord, I thank You for bringing me to a saving knowledge of You and Your Son, Jesus Christ. Thank You for bringing me up and out of captivity, and for saving me from bondage and slavery that the enemy brings. Through the precious name of Jesus, Amen.

Where is Love?
PART III - Calling
Chapter 7

Romans 8:28 And we know that in all things, God works for the good of those who love him, who have been called according to his purpose.

As I reflect on my life, I see how everything truly does work for good. God can take tragedy and make the ultimate outcome a positive one. That does not mean we will not suffer in the meantime, but God's aims are different from ours. We think we are here to achieve happiness, but God has holiness in mind as our primary goal.

When bad things knock us down, we have a choice. We can be bitter over a tragic situation or we can become better by enduring trouble and trusting God. He wants us to line up with His plan for us because it is a much better plan. As young people we often wonder: Why am I here? Just who am I in the scheme of things? Have you heard the story of the tapestry? We look at the "wrong" side of a weaver's project and see all the loose threads and the mess. Sometimes our lives look like messes. But as He works in our lives, He is creating a lovely scene on the front side of that tapestry. He knows just exactly how to put it all together and make something profoundly beautiful. Then we can glorify Him and show Christ to those around us.

Let's take a look at how God directed the life of Moses. You remember, he started out in a little basket, floating in the Nile River in Egypt. Pharaoh, the king, had decreed that all boy babies born to Israelite mothers were to be killed upon birth. Moses' mother wanted to save him, and she put him in a basket to float on the river. His sister was to watch and see what would happen. Pharaoh's daughter saw him, retrieved him as her own, and unknowingly hired his own mother to nurse him. He grew up in the palace and learned all that he would need later on to lead his people. But before that he remembered his mother and his family and so wanted to help them. He fought with an Egyptian and killed him. The only thing for Moses to do was disappear into the desert. It took 40 years for him to know what God wanted from him, and that was when he saw the burning bush and heard God's call. Subsequently Moses led his people out of Egypt, away from the crushing mandates of Pharaoh.

God may use others to work His plan for us. He has dreams and a future for all of us, and in due time they will all fit together like a completed puzzle. His way of looking at things is very different from ours. He is already into tomorrow and eternity. He sees us today not as we are now but what we will be. I am grateful that He is in the miracle business. He truly does want to line up our dreams with His; He is the dream maker. (Of course the enemy is the dream breaker and he does all he can to keep us from fulfilling our dreams.)

If you meditate on that verse in Romans (above), you see that we need to love Him. What must we do to show that we love Him? The Bible says we are to love Him with all our hearts, minds, souls and strength. The Bible tells us that over and over in various ways.

In *The Purpose Driven Life*, Rick Warren points out that we were created to have a relationship with God and to worship Him. He goes on to say that worship takes place not only in church, but we worship Him with our lives. That would be fulfilling His purpose. We are not here accidentally, we are not just blobs of nothing as the world and the enemy would have us believe. We truly are as unique as snowflakes and each of us is very special. We each have different life experiences, making us even more unusual. He personally knit us together before we were born. He has wonderful dreams and plans for us. And He has a calling for each of us.

Listen to His words as you each read the Bible. Practice obedience because, just as in any career or profession or skill, we need to study our textbook, the Bible. It contains directions for life. In a way it is a "road map". We are here as sojourners, travelers. God's Word points the way.

We have different roles to play and we have varied personalities but put all together, we have a well-rounded body of Christ, which we call the church. When I was young, I dreamed of being wife, mother, artist and speaker. I wanted to have close friends and be of use to mankind. I would have to say that God is well on His way to fulfilling all of those dreams for me.

One day about twenty-eight years ago as I was walking for exercise, God put a thought on my heart to write a book sometime. But I did not feel like doing it just then. Now here I am, years later, fulfilling His dream and mine, too. He let it grow in me and let me experience more of life so that this book could be of more value to the reader.

God did another special thing to help me with this book. Just before my mother was called home to Heaven, I met Bea, an editor/writer/teacher. She filled an empty space in my heart, and we have been prayer partners for several years. We pray together on Fridays for our church, our families, our country and of course, this book. The verse at the beginning of this chapter ("... all things work together for our good....") also says, "... we have been called to His purpose." Can you believe that? You and I have been called to His purpose.

Jesus is our role model, teaching us the way to respond to God's call. As we consider His example, on the surface it seems unfair that He came to die. Why did He die? Because He was obedient and did His Father's will. And we can benefit from that if we choose Him and His plan of Salvation. What does our purpose include? One thing we all can do is to share our faith and bring others to trust in Christ. If we don't do that, many will fail to find His plan and will miss Heaven.

We are in a battle, and we have a purpose. I want to fulfill mine. Every day I sing, "Lord Prepare Me To Be a Sanctuary..." I want to be His living sanctuary, where

God's Holy Spirit can live. In the New Testament the Holy Spirit is referred to as a gift, and He truly is. He will not leave us here alone.

Ever since I became a Christian, my goal has been to hear Jesus say, as I enter Heaven, "Well done, thou good and faithful servant." I can still remember sitting in front of my dad talking about my first pregnancy. This was before I was married. I cried, and I felt very ashamed. I don't want to feel that way when I stand before Christ.

We are all part of the body of Christ, the church. As every foot is needed, so is every hand, or mouth or eye. Whatever your function, do it willingly. Every part is vitally important to the body of Christ.

Following God's way can be exciting, surprising and fulfilling. God bless you as you search it out. I remember when I went on my first trip to help the missionaries in Ecuador. I was to give the children an art lesson. The children gathered around me as I sketched in the outline of a mural on the wall of a drab cement block building. It served as a school where 20 children attended in grades one to six.

They were intent on what I was planning to portray. It was Jesus seated on a bench with little ones gathered around. When it was finished but still just a sketch, the children could see what it was intended to be. They smiled and chattered. I did not know their language and they didn't know mine, but we communicated through exclamations and big smiles.

When I finally finished the sketching part and got the colors opened, their eyes grew large. I handed a brush to a tall boy and to an older girl. I indicated the correct color and the place to begin their strokes. They concentrated as though they were doing a math puzzle. Obviously they had not painted anything in their entire lives! Soon though they were busy dipping their brushes with increasing confidence. The others, who had been quiet at first, began to clamor for a turn. We worked all through the morning. All had painted; the shorter and younger children worked near the bottom of the scene. The mural had come to life and they were happy. The community looked very pleased and knew enough English to say "Thank you."

In a few days we flew out of the jungle, but our colorful gift would not be easily forgotten, a tangible reminder of Jesus' love for them all. We took with us one boy who was very sick, and also an adult native to accompany him. It could be scary to the child to be alone and without a familiar adult. These two were about to enter a totally new and different culture. We delivered them to one of the hospitals at the edge of the jungle.

God has allowed me to go to other countries and help the missionaries there. I have painted murals on schools and churches across South America and in Central America. At one time I thought painting was a waste of time, but God showed me how I could use my talent to encourage others, people whose languages I could not even speak. So, if you think your life is boring and has no meaning, think again. Find God's purpose for you and do it with all your heart. Have you made Him Lord of your life? Talk to Him, ask Him to show you His dreams for you. You will go on an adventure that you won't believe.

God had a vision for Moses, too. Moses thought he could not speak well enough to be a leader. I believe he wished he could have an impact on people. God had brought him to the Pharaoh's palace with all its advantages. God had dreams for Moses. We are blessed because we can look back and see how God worked in Moses' life. He even allowed Moses to kill a man as he stuck up for his people. Then he escaped into the desert to hide. Was God preparing the way for Moses to learn how to live in the desert? If He did, it worked. Remember, later Moses led the Israelites for forty years in the desert! It was in the desert that God presented Himself and told Moses who He was,- The Great I Am.

It didn't pay for Jonah to try to thwart God's plan for his life, either. God let him sit and think as he was in the belly of the large fish. Fortunately, the fish spit him out. God gave Jonah another chance.

God also gave me another chance. I was headed down the wrong path. Are you going in the wrong direction? God has something special just for you. Don't be impatient. This book has taken years to become a reality. My art has taken years to develop, and my speaking ability didn't happen overnight. But I feel I am finally following God's plan and I am happy.

Father, thank you for calling us to Your purposes. Thank You for making all things, good and bad, work together for those who follow You. That proves that You truly love us. In Jesus' name we pray, Amen.

Where is Love?
Chapter 8

Galatians 5:1 It is for freedom that Christ has set us free. Stand firm then and do not let yourselves be burdened again to a yoke of slavery.

God loves you completely. He invites your soul, your friendship and your worship. Part of His reason for loving you is to free you from bondage to Satan and to your own carnal nature. He allowed His Son to live here on earth with us and to die on that cross for you. God wants you to have the ultimate best in life.

I believe that from the time of birth we are slaves to our human nature. That dates back to the error made by Adam and Eve when they disobeyed God. We are for self only. It comes naturally. For example, do you see little children just naturally sharing with their siblings? No way. And even as grownups we will struggle to keep that which we have away from others. That is, before we see the light, through Christ.

I refer back to those 15-year-old boys who wanted sex with me. They were totally selfish, wanting only to gain pleasure for themselves, not caring about taking my virginity from me. Their own humanity was controlled by Satan and their flesh. That is not what God wants for any of us. He wants us to be family, caring about each other. And He wants us to have a personal relationship with Him through Christ Jesus. Without that, we are unhappy and miserable, letting Satan control us.

There are definitely two camps into which we may fall. One is Satan's, the other God's. Satan is all for death and destruction. God offers freedom. We have a choice: which one is going to rule us? If we want freedom to live out God's plan for us, we must choose Jesus.

God wants the very best for you. He wants to hear from you, to have fellowship with you, and He wants you to enjoy all that is in His blueprint for you. Satan, on the other hand, wants to sabotage God's wonderful plan for each of us.

Satan knows we are creatures of habit, and so we need to be very careful what we get involved with because it could become a bad habit. Ask any smoker if he can quit smoking. He/she may laugh and say, "Sure I can. I have quit many times." Ask a drug addict if he can quit on his own. He has a bad habit and it is so ingrained he no longer has control over it. Satan rules him.

I do not want to be enslaved to any thing that would keep me from God. Our sins do separate us from Him. However, if we know Him well, we can ask for forgiveness and He gives it.

Jesus told His followers to stand firm. Jesus was a wonderful role model for that. When He was being beaten, slapped and ridiculed, He never hit back, not even with words. He let God handle it. At one place in the Bible, we read about Daniel. He was dragged off as a teenager to Babylon, where life was about as ungodly as it could get. But Daniel refused to bow down to the king. He continued to pray to God. Because Daniel resisted the king's decree, because of his desire to remain strong, he was thrown into the lion's den. As you recall, the lion did not even touch Daniel; he was miraculously saved.

God is able to rescue us, too. I can remember several times in my life where God spared me from bad decisions, terrible accidents and my own foolishness. He rescued me. When Jesus was tempted by Satan during the forty days in the wilderness, He always answered the devil with scripture. If we know the Bible, we can do that, too. Think of the Bible as God's love letter to us, and it contains answers to many of life's choices. Learn from it.

Did I miss out on anything because of my rebellion and wrong choices? You bet I did. But I did not know how to ask for His help. I believe if I had been taught to trust God, things in my life would have been much different, much better.

We have all done things wrong and known the guilt and shame that follow. We hate to have our parents know what we have done wrong. A good parent knows he must warn a child about a hot stove. Touching it would burn him badly and leave a scar for life. God's help can keep us from acquiring many scars.

Once we are walking free, we never want to go back to slavery, to sin and destruction.

I have walked with God now for 30 years. I have not always done the right thing, and my life has not been a bowl of cherries. But I cannot imagine being without God. Everyone is going to experience difficulties and hardships. God sometimes allows that so we will grow to be the person God intended for us to be. During such times some people fall apart and go back to sinning. They stay in slavery or many times they turn back to slavery. It is the easier thing to do but God tells us to stand firm.

I recently saw Daryl Scott, father of Rachel Scott who was killed at Columbine High School where a classmate shot her. Her story reminds us to stand firm and be strong for God. Her murderers came to her and asked her twice if she believed in God. Each time she said "Yes," and they shot her both times. Her father tells her story so others can learn from her strength. She was true to God in the face of death. We may not face death as she did, but we often have to make decisions that require courage. Hold steady. God is in control.

We each have a choice: to be free and be our best self. Or we can miss the mark and make Satan our king and ultimately be a failure. Or we can use whatever gifts have been given to us so we can be a beacon in a dark world.

I can tell you from my experiences I know there is nothing better than to be used by God and to be doing what He has called me to do. Many times when I get up to speak for Him, to share my experiences, I know it is in His power and with His blessing. He is using me.

I am finally doing what He planned for me right from the beginning. There is so much freedom in that.

Many times God's ways are 100% the opposite from what we as humans think. At times young people believe that doing what they see as right is freedom. That is a lie from the devil. Freedom is doing what is right and what God has called us to do.

Father, thank You for leading me to freedom. Help me to stand firm and be strong, not falling back into sin and slavery. In Jesus' name, Amen

Where is Love?
Chapter 9

Ephesians 3:12 In Him and through faith in Him, we may approach God with freedom and confidence.

There is that word freedom again. We can come to Him in freedom and confidence. A little child can go to her daddy and say, "Daddy, my bike is broken and I can't fix it. You know how but I don't. Will you please help me?" She knows she can depend on her daddy for all of her needs. And as children grow up, they can ask for Dad's opinion or input; and Dad will offer his best advice and help them to think things through for the best solution. Of course all Christian dads will suggest the son or daughter consult God, too. Our parents are always on our team if we are going in the right direction.

God watches over us in even more ways than an earthly dad does. God can provide for us spiritually, and in fact already has. He sent Jesus to save us from our sins. All we have to do is accept that gift. God also provides for us in ways we do not always see. He will help you know what to do even as you grow up. He has written out directions for life in His love letter to us, the Holy Bible.

Why does God want to help us? Because He made us. He loves what He created; He wants us to be with Him in heaven. He has plans for us. And for each of you who reads this book, please find that plan and follow it. Jesus and His Father have a great future laid out for you. All you have to do is plug into it. God has all the wisdom, power, and love to help you with whatever is needed. He will help you be your very best. When you are obedient to God, you have all the power of heaven on your side. Just be sure you choose the plan that you are fitted for.

Jesus said we should pray to God for answers to all kinds of problems. God hears you and will help you. If you know the scriptures, you can follow instructions and be a winner. Is that going to be easy? Probably not. Even babies must struggle to learn to walk and talk. Part of God's plan for us involves using our fortitude, patience and hard work. These qualities are like muscles; they need to be used and exercised so those traits can grow into strong, sturdy parts of who and what we are.

Do you remember the Prodigal Son's story from the Bible? He went from his father's home and lived it up until his money ran out. He had almost nothing to eat. His only hope was to return to his father's home and be a worker in the fields. But he knew his dad well enough to know he would never turn his son away.

He was right. Instead of being lectured and scolded, he was greeted with open arms. He was given a royal robe and lots of food for a feast, and the father just could not quit rejoicing that his son had come home.

God is always in the "Daddy business", welcoming all who come to Him, even if they have sinned and done dumb things. No sinner is turned away if he or she comes with true repentance. Our earthly father's love for us cannot really compare to how much God loves each of us. He wants fellowship with you even though sin may get between you. Ask for forgiveness; and if you mean it, He will forgive. We have all sinned at one time or another but God does not throw us away. Just pick yourself up, repent, and ask for God's help.

Maybe you are thinking, why would God bother with us if we are sinners? The answer is in one word with four letters: Love.

We hear the word thrown around loosely and one out of ten times, it refers to mere infatuation or liking. God's love is far more. It is sacrificial. He sent Jesus to die on a painful rough cross with a crown of thorns on His head. Both God and Jesus loved you - yes, you - enough to buy you back from Satan.

Who is Satan? He is a mean, nasty, cruel, evil being who lies, cheats, steals and fools you into following him. He wants to control you, not give you freedom. He hates every one of us, especially those who are Christians. He is clever and can make sin look like something you just have to have or do. If you don't know God's way, the right way, you will fall for Satan's lies. He will have you in his trap.

A fine Christian speaker and writer, Beth Moore, wrote a book called (Get Out of That Pit). We fall into a trap because we are not thinking about it. Satan is gleeful when that happens. He hates Jesus and he hates you. If he can take you away from Jesus, he has scored a great victory for himself. He wants to take you to hell when you die. He knows that would hurt God and Jesus.

Maybe we should be more specific about the way Satan works. Let's say you know a lot of kids in school who are either on drugs or selling them. They want you to join them. They may even give you some "crack" to sample. You really would like to know what there is about that drug that makes people use it. Would one little sample get you hooked? You may tell yourself you are only looking for information so you can understand drug addicts and help them.

Whoa! You are rationalizing. You are being sold false info. The Bible says ask Jesus for help NOW. Think of what you are doing. You could be hooked for life with just one drug dose. It is wrong to abuse your body. Pray for God to help you, and He will. You will have exercised will power, you have said "No" to Satan. Quote a Bible verse to him, and he will flee from you.

I am sure you could think of many other times that you are tempted to fall into the pit. The same principles apply. Gather your courage and say No.

You can make a decision right now. Choose Jesus, and you will spend eternity in heaven. If you do not choose Jesus, you have automatically put yourself on Satan's side. To not make a choice means you have chosen Hell as your home for all of eternity.

What are the advantages in belonging to Jesus? 1. He loves you and will not send harm to you, ever. 2. He is available to you through prayer 24/7. 3. God can do anything. No problem is too big. 4. You can give any problem to God and then rest. He is able. 5. He knows the future and can guide you in everything.

Obviously, God is the best choice you can make. But do not expect Him to push you into the Christian life. It is your choice. He wants His children to come to Him because they love and respect Him; He doesn't want just puppets.

The decision is yours. You may disagree with God at times, but keep in mind, He has been around for a very long time and knows what is best for you. Poor choices can lead to problems. Then Satan is gleeful.

Remember what we said about strengthening a muscle. Patience and fortitude also strengthen when they are used.

If this sounds as though trouble makes you stronger, it really does. And it also draws us closer to God. It is well for us to keep in mind that our enemy, Satan, is evil all the way through. He makes forbidden things look desirable, but do not be deceived.

I am not writing about life just from a"rules" point of view. God wants our obedience to Him to be out of love, not just rules. I have experienced the nasty things Satan will tell us. He has told me personally that I am of no value, that I am ugly and stupid and undesirable. It is easy to believe him if our guard is down. But when you realize that God sent His only Son to die for you - yes, you - it makes you aware that God considers you super special. You can "take that to the bank".

Things happen sometimes that do not seem good. Your mom or dad would not let you eat a dozen green apples. They know what it would do to you.

But if you sneak around and eat them, you would be making a wrong choice, and you will no doubt regret it. You did it to yourself. Your parents are sorry for you as you throw up apples, but you made a wrong choice. They still love you, though. Likewise, God loves you unconditionally. He never quits loving you.

I don't have to tell you we have all made mistakes. When that happens, you don't feel free any more. You don't feel free or in control. You have let Satan sneak in, and he is happy to see you fail. Just remember, anything the devil wants for you will hurt you. He is just naturally evil, all the way through.

However, the great gift of love which God has given us is more precious than we can understand.

Now, I, Cindy, have gone through a lot, as this story has already shown you. I have made many poor choices. Satan's lies are seductive. Many times I have failed to keep that in mind. I have paid a big price for my disobedience. Let's look at the differences between what God wants for us and what Satan wants. I made a little chart for you to fill in showing in black and white the call Satan makes to you and what God's calling is. Think about each category mentioned and note the differences.

Satan Wants	God Wants
Sex before marriage	Pure Intimate Bond
Using illegal drug	Healthy Mind and Body
Risking STDs	Waiting for Marriage
Ignoring your curfew	Respecting Authority
Lying to your Parents	Honor Your Parents

Which side are you on? You get the idea, I'm sure.

Dear God, help me to be wise enough to follow the way You have laid out for me to follow. Help me to be alert to Satan's trap. Help me fulfill the role You designed me for. In Jesus' name, Amen

Where is Love?
Chapter 10

Matthew 28:18-20 Jesus came and told his disciples, all authority in heaven and on earth has been given to me. Go and make disciples of all nations. Baptize them in the name of the Father and the Son and the Holy Spirit. Teach these new disciples to obey all the commands I have given you. And be sure of this: I am with you always even to the end of the age.

Jesus spoke these words to His disciples and also to you and me. You remember our third section of this book is labeled "calling". God is calling you to a ministry of your own. It is no accident that you are reading this book at this point in your life. The challenge is to you: "Go." Each of the four gospels ends with this command to spread the word, the Good News of Jesus Christ. The basic message will be the same, but we will all have a certain way of expressing it. If you watch Christian TV, you will find that each preacher/speaker has his own "spin" on the gospel. That is, each expresses it through his own set of experiences. Some people are drawn to one evangelist, and some to others. There is a variety of presentations. However, the core message is the same: Jesus Saves.

It is interesting to note that the first two letters in the word "God" say "Go". The first three letters in "Satan" spell "sat". Satan does not want the word of God to be spread around.

We mentioned earlier the story of Jonah. Jonah had been commissioned to go to Ninevah and carry the message of God to the people there. It was a message of loving warning with a promise of good to come if the people would change their wicked ways. God purposely chose Jonah to carry this message. He knew Jonah hated the Ninevites, and it would be a stretch for him to give good news to Ninevah. Isn't that just like God? He gave Jonah a chance to grow, to grow out of disobedience and hatred into doing God's bidding. It was a tough lesson for Jonah, but he found it is best to respond to God's calling promptly.

You too have a calling, a purpose to fulfill. It is as tailored to your own circumstances as Jonah's was. That is exciting! Your story is built exactly to specifications for His plan for you. There are people who will respond to your message of hope because it connects them to some of their own experiences. Just be yourself, and the message will register.

Often, as I walk around my house and yard, I sing to myself. My favorite song is, "Something beautiful..." It goes, "Something beautiful, something good, all my confusion You understood."

He will put you in a place where you will be most effective, where your story is needed. When you can give a person new hope, it is a joy. And to tell them they are okay and God loves them, it gladdens your heart, too.

One day when I was out walking I saw a butterfly, floating on the breeze. It gave me a God thought. That is how free we are when we trust in Jesus. It reminded me that in the beginning of its life, the butterfly was just a pokey little caterpillar. He was limited in what he could do or how far he could go. But once he emerged from his cocoon, he spread his beautiful wings and flew into the air, no longer limited. Think of your mission this way: you can help other "caterpillars" become beautiful butterflies by telling the story of Jesus.

My husband has always planned his life by setting goals. It worked for him, so a few years ago I wrote out a Mission Statement for myself. That helps me stay focused. Do you have direction for your life? Do you have a sense that you are going in the right direction?

Each morning when I get up I say, "Thank you God for loving me." Then I ask Him to fill me with His Holy Spirit. I know I am nothing without Him, that I can only accomplish things by calling on His great power. He is calling you and me to obedience. Go and share the Good News!

Dear Lord, Open our eyes to the opportunities all around us where we can share the Good News of Jesus. Help us find and live out the original purpose which You have for us. Thanks for loving us so much that You sent Your Son to save us. Your love is incredible, and we are grateful to have it shine on us. We pray this in the name of Jesus, Amen.

Epilogue

Beloved,yes you, that is how God sees you. As I finish this book I am going through a very painful time in my life. I am doing well, I have my moments but God is showing His Power and Love throughout the circumstances. This is the whole reason for this book; who is your True Love? Mine is My Heavenly Father and because of that and the relationship I have developed with Him I am okay and He is being Glorified. I know there are purposes for what I am going through and He and I will find ways to use it. It will not be for naught or wasted. I love the phrase, "Life is hard but....GOD IS GOOD"!!!!

Develop your relationship with Him, run after Him, seek Him in anyway you can. Then and only then will you have joy in pain, strength in the storms and purpose no matter what. The good times will be bonuses and everything will fit into place in this fallen world where the prince of darkness wants to keep you from any peace, love, and joy. The God of the universe brings meaning to your life and He will help you to fulfill your dreams.

As I close may I pray for you one last time? *My Heavenly Father, bless this young reader with a solid growing relationship with You. May she see purpose and Your Presence in both good and bad times. Help her to work at her dreams and help her to wait for Your direction in her choice of a husband. Bring one that also has a solid relationship with You. May she always remember that she is Your Treasured Possession. Send her a husband worth waiting for. In Jesus Name, Amen.*

Blessings, Cindy

Dating Strategies

1. Have you asked God's guidance and direction?

2. Are you aware of any family baggage [dysfunctions] you may have that could hurt a relationship?

3. Do you know how to work through a conflict creatively not aggressively and does he?

4. Have you developed a close relationship with the Author of Love, learning His ways of love?

5. Have you learned to be respectful of other people?

6. Are you aware of who you are and secure in that?

7. Have you spent adequate time in group settings with peers to learn to communicate and have fun with guys?

8. This is a huge decision to date are you ready, you will very likely get your heart broken if you're too young.

9. Take a good hard look at the other person in these areas too.

10. Does he know God and seek more of Him?

11. How does he interact with his mother does he respect her? This is where her learned to respect women.

12. How about writing a list a good qualities that you would like in a husband and father for your future.

LaVergne, TN USA
24 September 2010
198307LV00002B/3/P